T0086506

# WHISPERS IN THE WIND

## THE POETRY WHISPERER

### SHIRLEY SECURRO

authorHOUSE®

*AuthorHouse*™
*1663 Liberty Drive*
*Bloomington, IN 47403*
*www.authorhouse.com*
*Phone: 1 (800) 839-8640*

© *2017 Shirley Securro. All rights reserved.*

*No part of this book may be reproduced, stored in a retrieval system, or*
*transmitted by any means without the written permission of the author.*

*Published by AuthorHouse   06/30/2017*

*ISBN: 978-1-5246-9773-0 (sc)*
*ISBN: 978-1-5246-9772-3 (e)*

*Library of Congress Control Number: 2017910084*

*Print information available on the last page.*

*Any people depicted in stock imagery provided by Thinkstock are models,*
*and such images are being used for illustrative purposes only.*
*Certain stock imagery © Thinkstock.*

*This book is printed on acid-free paper.*

*Because of the dynamic nature of the Internet, any web addresses or links contained in*
*this book may have changed since publication and may no longer be valid. The views*
*expressed in this work are solely those of the author and do not necessarily reflect the views*
*of the publisher, and the publisher hereby disclaims any responsibility for them.*

*New Living Translation (NLT)*
*Holy Bible, New Living Translation, copyright © 1996, 2004, 2015*
*by Tyndale House Foundation. Used by permission of Tyndale House*
*Publishers Inc., Carol Stream, Illinois 60188. All rights reserved.*

*King James Version (KJV)*
*Public Domain*

*The Message (MSG)*
*Copyright © 1993, 1994, 1995, 1996, 2000, 2001, 2002 by Eugene H. Peterson*

*New International Version (NIV)*
*Holy Bible, New International Version*®*, NIV*® *Copyright ©1973, 1978, 1984,*
*2011 by Biblica, Inc.*® *Used by permission. All rights reserved worldwide.*

*English Standard Version (ESV)*
*The Holy Bible, English Standard Version. ESV*® *Permanent Text Edition*® *(2016).*
*Copyright © 2001 by Crossway Bibles, a publishing ministry of Good News Publishers.*

# ACKNOWLEDGEMENT

I thank my Heavenly Father for giving me the gift of poetry. I have written poetry since the age of 10, but the gift of spiritual poetry was given to me approximately 14 years ago. I got spiritual poetry about the sermon after church one Sunday on the way home and had to pull the car over to the side of the road to write it down. That was my first experience with spiritual poetry, and I had it published. COME BEFORE WINTER was the name of the sermon that day and also the name of my poetry. Winter is when things die and we are to do things for the Kingdom while we are still here on this earth. Our time here on this earth is very short.

# ABOUT THE BOOK

**Whispers in the Wind-*The Poetry Whisperer*** is a collection of poetry that was written to be a source of inspiration. Poetry tells a story, and you will be delighted at the stories in this book that are written in an easy-to-understand style. This book offers hope and healing with insight into the world around us. I have written about our American heroes, nature, our losses, our tears, forgiveness to those who have hurt us, giving second chances (everyone deserves a second chance; give one or receive one), and whimsical writings for the lighthearted.

I have also written about angels, God, Jesus, Easter, and Christmas. There is a little romance, poetry for wedding vows, and several tributes.

# ABOUT SHIRLEY SECURRO

Shirley has a home ministry, Securro Ministries, where she has taught a weekly Bible School to children from the ages of 5 thru 12 and also adult Bible studies. She has been in leadership in three different churches. She has taught Sunday School, Bible School, Junior Church, Royal Rangers (was a Commander in the boy's club), a Teen Club, and adult Bible studies.

She attended the University of Akron and worked for a Fortune 500 Company for 23 years.

Shirley has been published in the following anthologies:

FAMOUS POETS OF THE HEARTLAND

LUCIDITY

ON GOSSAMAR WINGS

ON THE WINGS OF PEGASUS

POEMS OF BEAUTIFUL OHIO – THEN AND NOW (Illustrated the front cover and has several sketches in the book)

SONGS OF HONOUR

THEATRE OF THE MIND

THE BEST POEMS AND POETS OF 2005

THE INTERNATIONAL WHO'S WHO IN POETRY – 2005

THE INTERNATIONAL WHO'S WHO IN POETRY – 2007

TIMELESS VOICES

VOICES IN VERSE – WEAVING WORDS (along with several sketches)

MUSE AND VIEWS – A Kaleidoscope of Poetry – also compiled and edited for The Poet's Nook (The Poet's Corner)

Shirley has been published online on www.alongstoryshort, a writer's Ezine, LONG STORY SHORT magazine, POEMS OF THE WORLD, (this journal is sent around the world and to Universities in China to translate into Chinese since Shakespeare is too difficult for them to translate), and her poetry has been recorded on two different CD's (one that went around the world). She had her poetry, THE CHRISTMAS GIFT, published on a Christmas card. She was a finalist in a chapbook contest with "AMERICA – Let Freedom Reign, Our Sacrifices – Our Heroes." She is also an APPOINTED and REGISTERED United States Poetry Ambassador doing readings for churches, weddings, funerals, banquets, clubs, and meetings. Shirley enjoys teaching, reading, music, poetry, and sketching.

# CONTENTS

# ANGELS

Psalm 91:11 For He orders His angels to protect us wherever we go (NLT)
We have more than one!

# AN ANGEL'S JOY

The angels dance in the wind
We know not where or when

God's joy sends them on their way
and ours entices them to stay

Our joy propels them
to take flight and return again

To an angel joy is energy
God's and ours is synergy

# ANGELS IN FLIGHT

Angels in flight
The speed of light

The wind they ride
The Spirit's guide

Falling, drifting from above
Carried by invisible love

# HEAVENLY BEINGS

We need angels to help us love
Heaven sent from up above
Angels come down when we're in tears
I've known that throughout the years
In happiness as well as in sorrow
Necessary to meet our tomorrow
Angels come in any shape or size
so don't hesitate to recognize
when in each phase of life they're here
the end or beginning of each year
Angels are not selfish it seems
Magnificent "Heavenly Beings!"
Angels are blessings to us they give
Everything needed to love, laugh, and live!


Psalm 56:8 You keep track of all of my sorrows. You have collected all my tears in your bottle. You have recorded each one in your book. (NLT).

# THE RUFFLE OF WINGS

Light as a feather and quieter than snow
Angels are with us wherever we go
To lead us, to guide us, to protect us too
It's obvious they are here and I always knew
that they were sent from our Father above
full of His grace, His mercy, His love
They pick us up whenever we fall down
In the wrong direction they turn us around
When those who have wronged us we forgive
we get more angel power and love to live
Between robes, harps, haloes, and wings
what a wonder all of those heavenly things
Angels are an extension of God's hand
He stationed them everywhere in this land
His extraordinary presence they make known
The miracles and dreams we have been shown
The touch of an angel is like the warm sun
radiating down and encouraging them to run
beside, behind, before, above us in all ways
We are protected all around for all of our days
All of these angels around me I long to see
especially the ones assigned to protect me!
So be gentle with those who come your way
It could be your guardian angels assigned to stay!

Published in VOICES in VERSE WEAVING WORDS
Published in The International WHO'S WHO IN POETRY, 2007

# GENERAL

# A MOTHER

Nothing on this earth compares
with the love of a mother who cares

The sun, the moon, the stars above
the magnitude of all her love

A mother, a rose, a garden flower
refreshes like a summer shower!

Published in Long Story Short Magazine

# ACCEPTANCE

Why do we think we have to be liked
by everyone who comes our way?
Those who leave us and the ones who stay?
Some people are moody and unhappy at best
forget those people and love the rest!
Try to find your niche like a bird in a nest
We try to love the unlovable
and it only results in trouble
Unhappy people stir up the pot
whether you accept them or not!
In all kinds of weather they're always the same
They seem to be looking for someone to blame
They don't like your skills or gifts
and constantly causing rifts
So move along and find the ones to accept
who are looking for people to connect!

# A LEADER

When you lead a group
you're under a microscope
and it isn't always easy to cope
Some go and some stay
It's always been that way
Some look for flaws
Just because
they are mad
they need to get glad!
To have someone
who leads and shares
to carry the burden who cares
Ignore the bad and take the good
and keep our spirits up we should!
It won't be long
before they're gone
We need to take a second look!

# AMBITION

Ambition is a powerful drive;
it can keep all of us alive.
Ambition can soar like the eagles;
great minds are carried on its wings.
It can keep you up at night.
It's self-discipline on a flight.
It's like the butterfly effect: changes take place,
discoveries are made, lives are saved.
Climb with ambition to reach the top.
Don't let it die, keep it alive, let it survive!
Don't let it creep like you are asleep.
It must be higher than you are.
Ambition gets you through the door.
Be ambitious of true honor.
Reach the stars with your ambition,
or with your ability.
It may be a blessed chance to shine
It's the drive that's kept alive.
Look ahead and not behind.
We are capable of greater things.

Published in MUSE AND VIEWS – A Kaleidoscope of Poetry and POEMS OF THE WORLD

# A TRUE FRIEND

Friends come in all shapes and sizes
Some disappoint and some surprise us
Love the ones who love you
they're bound to be faithful and true
Be honest and caring and always sharing
When things go wrong they'll be around
they're a soft place to fall ready to answer your call
to share a tear or two
Keep the ones who lift you
A true friend will be by your side
closer than family, will always abide
True friends aren't as plentiful as they used to be
I need to hold on to the ones around me
They've moved, they've died
And, yes, I've cried
to lose the ones I held dear
Some far away, few are near
To forever lose a friend
takes time to be happy again!

Published in POEMS OF THE WORLD

# BLESS US AGAIN LORD

We're out to sea without an anchor
Lord, please don't let us go
The Bible is your Holy Book
It shows us how to grow
Without your grace where would we be?
Why can't Americans stop to see?
We're in a downward spiral
I know why this has to be
Because of murder, anger, violence escalating
We're drowning out at sea
We've taken you out of everything
And America used to be
Blessed by you in every way
No longer can we say
We are the best, we honor you
Are we still the red, white & blue?
You will come back and protect us
If only we would stay true
To the Holy God who blessed us so
In everything that we do!

# BOSTON LIGHT

(Lighthouse)
The lighthouse is a friend to a sailor
always warning him of peril and danger
It could be a tower, or short with a bright light
Smoke could be seen by day, or the light by night
They are traffic signs for those on the sea
Traveling by water seemed the place to be
Navigation is travel by sea on a boat
The people needed guidance to stay afloat
The history of that bright shining light
kept people safe throughout their plight
from going down into depths unknown
That brilliant light we have been shown
There have been different shapes and colors,
but one stands out above the automated others
It's on Little Brewster Island named "Boston Light"
The only one left manned by keepers to keep it right

Boston Light was the last lighthouse to be automated and manned by keepers for sentimental reasons and the first one built on the shores of the free! Boston Light was built in 1716 and destroyed in the American Revolutionary War. It was rebuilt in 1783 and has stood for over 200 years. In 1964 it was named a National Historic landmark.

# CRITICISM

Criticism is not a good thing to do
especially when someone works free for you
You stepped right up to the plate
holding on to that past mistake
to blurt out your distaste

Knowing there are typos in every book
Just go to the library and take a look!
Appreciate when others give of their time
trying to make things for you sublime

Did you find fault with others to their face?
Did you let them know your distaste?
To find fault is to criticize
When will you ever realize?
Sit back, judge, find fault if you dare
You might just fall on your face with flair!

# DECEPTION

I'm looking for honesty
A lost virtue, obscure
It's like looking
for a needle in a haystack

Eluding each corner
Of my existence
Seeking the truth at
each bend in the road
I'm living in a forest of deception

An age of deception
Grasping, hoping,
Drowning in a sea of despair!

Darkness all around
Falsehoods
My disappointments
Just be honest!

# DECISIONS

Decisions fill my life in every way
I need to make them every day
Should I go or should I stay?

Get married? Stay single?
Isolate myself or mingle?

Search for my knight in shining armor?
Is there such a man? I'll always wonder

Good decisions take a lot of thought
Weight everything carefully
Think before you speak
Make strong decisions not weak

Lighten the load of a person in need
That decision results in a very good deed!

# FLY AWAY

Let your heart take wings and fly
Up into the beautiful sky
Where the musical birds reside
Leave your worries and cares behind
Just for a moment in time
Those who tear you down
Leave them all around
Why do they dislike you so?
There is a better way to go
Unhappy, unsatisfied are they
That's why you simply can't stay
In their small perspective of you
You tried to show them "The Way"
True love from above
They just couldn't see
What was meant to be
You can be so nice to them
You can try your best to win
They're not on your side
They just don't want to abide
Let your heart take wings and fly
Up into the beautiful sky!

John 14:6 Jesus told him, "I am the way, the truth, and the life." (NLT)

# FRIENDS

When a friend disappoints you
try not to be too blue
It's their weakness showing through
They are disappointed with life
and seem so full of strife
Just give it a rest
and look to their best
We all have bad days
It may just be a phase
We need to decide
Is it worth it to abide?
Should we bail this person out
time after time?
That is the question we must decide
What does this friendship add to our life?

# HAPPINESS

Dip your toe into the pool of happiness
Don't be afraid to drown
It might just turn your life around
Turn your frown upside down
Think on things that are true and good
Is what everyone should
Be the positive one who cares
And always be the one who shares
Look up above and not below
Be quick about it
And don't be too slow
Get off of that boat of negativity
It makes us as unhappy as we can be
And don't forget to forgive quickly!
Negative thoughts destroy our DNA
We sure don't want to go that way
Forget the past it doesn't last
Look forward to the best
Just pass that test
Jump instead on the train of love
All love is sent down from above!

# HAVE MERCY

Have mercy on us Lord
And take us thru this storm
It's coming very soon
There's no stopping this typhoon

We've turned our backs on you
We're counting you'll see us through
Natural disasters are on the rise
You said to look to the skies

We've gone our separate ways
We've forgotten you for days
The time is short, we can come clean
Repent, forgive and start again

2 Chronicles 7:14 Then if my people who are called by my name will humble themselves and pray and seek my face and turn from their wicked ways, I will hear from heaven and forgive their sins and heal their land. (NLT)

# HIDDEN PLACES OF THE HEART

Hidden places of the heart
We all have them
Mother, Father, Siblings
First day of school
God
Happiness, Pets
First boyfriend, first kiss
Best friend
Graduation Day, college
Career
Engagement
Wedding day
Betrayal
Birth of a baby
Joy
Disappointments
Death of loved ones
Grief
Child's wedding
Birth of a grandchild
These occasions will always be

# HIDDEN PLACES OF THE HEART

# KING OF KINGS AND LORD OF LORDS

Heal our land Lord I pray
I cry to you night and day
The sin is abounding everywhere
In the city, the country, even the air

Must they kill those who protect and serve?
It's happening every day
When will this end, or is it here to stay?
Why can't the masses learn?
We don't honor you
We've turned our backs on what is good

Where has the love gone?
The greatest commandment of all
Was it like this before the fall?
Can we make a change, or is it too late
Will this be our country's fate?

Will it get worse? Are we under a curse?
It's time to show the world
That you're the Mighty Lord!
That you are King of the land
And you have a mighty hand
I pray you see us through when it starts to begin
The seas will roar, the mountains fall
You'll show the world your power once for all!

The prophet, Jeremiah, expressed his grief, sorrow & tears over the sinfulness of the Israelites. The people of Israel had chosen to reject God. Jeremiah 4: 1 & 2 "O Israel, come back to me," says the LORD. "If you will throw away your detestable idols and go astray no more, and if you will swear by my name alone, and begin to live good, honest lives and uphold justice, then you will be a blessing to the nations of the world, and all people will come and praise my name."

# MEAN PEOPLE

Mean people are all around
They're unhappy I have found
They like to attack
You shouldn't fight back
Don't fall into that trap!
They try to cause discord
I have seen it before
No matter who they offend
At times even a friend
It never seems to end
Friendships are lost
At such a high cost
The easiest way is to chime in
There is no way to win
With hurt angry words
Just turn from them
Stay out of their way
until you can pray
We have to forgive!

# OPINIONS

Opinions are based on tried and true
They are a part of me, a part of you
No opinion you state is ever wrong
It compares to singing your very own song
Research your subject before you speak
Keep the atmosphere light not to be bleak
Opinions are what you stringently believe
It's best to state them in order to relieve
At times you hold back not to discord
The feelings of others kept in accord
You know when it's best just to remain
Quiet when only in your own domain
Others refrain when you become vocal
Just humble yourself not to be focal
So keep the peace wherever you go
Learn to know when to take it slow
No two opinions alike I'm happy to say
Just be bold, give it anyway
Respect other's opinions whatever they be
We are all a part of God's family


Published in MUSE AND VIEWS – A Kaleidoscope of Poetry

# OUR WORLD TODAY

There is so much pain and suffering in our world today
Where can we possibly go to get away?
To another planet by space travel?
Before we all completely unravel?
It's better to stay and make this place
safer with peace for the whole human race
To feed the hungry, to clothe the poor
To help each person who arrives at our door
It's what we're called to do each day
It's how our Heavenly Father says is the way
If we each would obey and do what is right
It would be acceptable in God's sight
To do our share just to show we care
Can bring peace and happiness everywhere
To put others first the way that we should
Would be the best thing if everyone would
The evil is all around us everywhere
Maybe it's because we just don't share
The love of God that we've been given
By our Heavenly Father who is up in heaven
Make the change for others to see
By action and speech and also in deed
Is exactly what this world may need!

# SCHOOL

When I was young and went to school
The teacher taught the Golden Rule
"Sit up straight and bow your head
It's time to have the prayer read
Fold your hands and close your eyes"
Many times we would hear her sighs
"We need to ask our Father above
To teach us all about His love
to keep us pure and not to lie
To be honest and true to get us by"
She would announce loud and clear
And if you pretended not to hear
She didn't hesitate to tug your ear
It wasn't considered child abuse then
It was all about why we should and when
The Bible was the ruling force
We went to Sunday School of course
Things were different times gone by
I can still hear those teachers sigh!

# SECOND CHANCES

Second Chances
We all need them
We all desire them
We all get them
Take advantage
They are right
Around the corner
Lurking
Don't let them
Pass you by
Give the gift
Forget the past
See the new
Take the risk
Watch it change
For the best
Change your mind
Turn your heart
Make it right
Accept the gift
Mend the rift

# SECOND CHANCES

# SECRETS

Everyone has a secret
Too private to share

Something too sacred
Wanting to escape

Clearly never to dare!

## SECRETS

# THE HOUSE ON BAY STREET

When I pass by the house on Bay Street
At twilight it's always a treat!
The beautiful candles in the windows
Are always lit
And at times I just stop and sit
The candles are luminous, colorful, and bright
As they light up the neighborhood
It's a beautiful sight!
Every window has one in place
Almost looking like someone's face
The house on Bay Street has a warm beckoning vibe
That house almost seems to be alive
Where there is always laughter filling the air
And people milling around everywhere
Cars, RV's, vans, cycles and bikes to race
Adding to the personality of that place
If the house could speak what would it say?
Would it beckon me to go on my way?
Or would it welcome me with greetings of the day?
Would it tell me of the love that flows inside and out
And the hopes and dreams spilling about?
I think it would tell me that it was very much
loved, cherished, and respected!

# THE HOUSE ON BAY STREET

32

# THE DAYS OF INNOCENCE

Gone is the innocence of my yesterdays
They are forever etched in time in all ways
They were precious and lasting
The days that were passing and
Now all of that is left behind
Lost in time, but always in mind

To bring out on days when needed
Thank God that he has them seeded
A place to be nurtured and fed
Deep in my soul and in my head
I bring out the innocence that I once knew
At times when needed, at times out of the blue

Those days of innocence will always be mine
They are safe and sound and where I can find
I can remember the laughter, the smiles, and the love
All of these things sent down from above
The love of family that surrounded all around
I look and pursue and finally have found
That same kind of love somewhere to be
It's bigger and unconditional and all around me
It's the love from my Heavenly Father above
It dame down from heaven light as a dove
I can go on now because His love abounds
It's comforting and nurturing and always surrounds!

Published in MUSE AND VIEWS – A Kaleidoscope of Poetry

# THE DAYS OF MY YOUTH

The days of my youth were the best for me
They will forever be precious in my memory
The sweet days of summer and spring and fall
I remember so clearly every one of them all

My neighbors, my teachers, my friends galore
Now scattered all over from shore to shore
The people were different way back then
They had so much character and much less sin

We were taught what was wrong and what was right
It was acceptable and agreed to in everyone's sight
People were caring, giving, and happy too
They were a lot like me and a lot like you

It was a great time to be alive
And to those of us who did survive
We didn't have to lock our doors at night
Even in the dark where there wasn't a light

We got lost in the neighborhood for days
The neighbors back then had caring ways
We always had room for friends at the table
We were all so healthy and willing and able
To help a friend in time of need
It still should be a very good deed

The days of my youth were the best that there were
Everything such an adventure so sweet and so pure
My youth was a time of laughter, innocence, and tears
I will always remember all of those years.

Published in The International WHO'S WHO IN POETRY, 2005

# THE WIND — FRIEND OR FOE?

My friend the wind
Where has it been?
I know not where or when
The mountain tops high
Or the valleys low
Very high speeds or slow
The wind on my face
Light and soft
Feelings of freedom
Not readily lost
The wind in a storm
Threatening at best
Electric lines down
Danger at rest
The wind in the night
Gives us a fright
Everyone safe
Or out on a flight?
The wind of a typhoon
Safe at home in my room
Lives lost
Homes destroyed
The deadly wind

# TOMORROW

Tomorrow what will you bring?
Happiness and a song to sing
A tear-filled day
That calls to pray?
Or none of these things?

Tomorrow what will you bring?
A boring hour
An exciting call
Dancing on toes
Without a fall
A friend to share
Someone to care
Or none of these things?

Tomorrow what will you bring?
A kind or loving word
A beautiful flying bird
A smile from a stranger
A flirt with danger
Or none of these things?

Tomorrow what will you bring?
A dream unmet
A promise kept
To be at rest
To hope for the best
Or none of these things?
Tomorrow what will you bring?

# WE ARE THE CHURCH

We are the church the people of God
Lift up your hands and applaud!
Jesus is the head our chief cornerstone
The battle over satan has been won!
All nature acknowledges him
He has power to forgive our sin
Glorify God with all you've got
Don't ever stop!
Glorify him in all you do
He will stay true
Daily if you need it
Just believe it!
Trust in the Lord with all your heart
And he will give you a brand new start!
The choice is up to you
His promises will see you through!


Ephesians 2:20 Together we are his house, built on the foundation of the apostles and the prophets and the cornerstone is Christ Jesus himself (NLT)

# WE GO ON

We mourn the things we lose
We're heavy with grief and despair
We survive by being in denial
And we go on

We laugh, we love, we live
We hurt, we cry, we forgive
We suffer and strive and survive
And we go on

We overlook, we overcome
We heal
And we go on

We stumble and fall and get up
We dream and we reach our goals
We rejoice!
And we go on

Published in POEMS OF THE WORLD

# WHAT HAVE WE DONE?

How can we say our country is safe?
With killings going on all over the place?
I pray daily to God to show us his grace
More innocent lambs murdered in each race
God hates the hands that shed innocent blood
We are being destroyed by fire, tornadoes and flood
We could have had two million more
Members of our society to be adored
They were murdered before being born
Another Washington, a doctor, a dedicated teacher?
Another Bach or even the right preacher?
Someone with wisdom to lead us and show the way
We'll never know what could have been to this day
Something for us to think about
Decisions to be made
Will we destroy or pave a new way?


Revelation 22:21 The grace of the Lord Jesus be with you all (NLT)

# WHAT'S IN A NAME?

Our name is who we are
Our name is what we are
Our name is our legacy
Our name is our heritage
Our name is our legal right
Our name says it all
Our name speaks volumes about us
Our name gets us in the door
Our name can be respected or rejected
Our name can be plain or beautiful
We stand behind our name
We are proud of our name
Our name has a meaning
There are thousands of names
Do you like your name? Do you rely on your name?
Or do you make your own way?
Does your name get you in the door?
Are people famous or are their names famous?
Are they the same? The person? The name?
What's in a name?
Everything is in a name if it is Washington, Lincoln, Kennedy
It's all about the name
We are our name!

# PROMISES

# ADAM AND EVE

Adam and Eve what have you done?
Because of your sin God sent His son!
To suffer and die on that cross
To save me and all of the lost!
To be at peace with Him again
And all because of your terrible sin!
You disobeyed the Master of the Universe
You fell and made our earth much worse!
We could have lived forever in this land,
But that was all changed by your hand!
God loved you so very much
That apple you had to touch!
To bring us all down, that's why we frown
At what you did that one single day
God made a way for us to pray
To ask forgiveness and pave the way
To accept Jesus His son
And breach the gap that you have done
When we do this He forgives our sins
And we can be at peace again!
Our happy home in heaven we'll be
Throughout eternity!

# AFFLICTION

When affliction comes your way
Always remember that you should pray
Ask the Lord to comfort you
Unlike man God is true blue
Hold tight to him and you will see
How faithful that the Lord can be
Remind him that you've kept the law
Above all else and did not fall
"Is anything too hard for me?" says the Lord
Remember past blessings that he has poured
He will do for you again what he did in the past
Remember those things so that they will last
Hold unto his promises every day
Remind him of what he did say
"You'll go thru the waters, but you won't drown"
Didn't he say he could turn anything around?
Do not complain and look to him
He can make things right again
Make melodies in your heart every day
And you will see the affliction go away
His word does not return void to him
Hallelujah! Praise God and Amen!

(Written from Pastor Caskey's sermon at Faith Baptist Church on Affliction)

# A PROMISE MADE

To sit at the window, to look at the trees
The squirrels, the birds, the warm summer breeze
To enjoy the blue sky, the smile of the sun
It won't be long before summer has gone
It's all about God and the beauty He's given
It's lasting, it's lingering, showered down from heaven
How can a person not believe? The seas, the moon, the stars
All of the galaxies, black holes, and Mars
Space above, the oxygen we breathe
All because of our basic need
To survive on this planet that we call earth
The place that we've all been birthed
A promise made, a promise to keep
When the times comes for us to sleep!

# CAIN AND ABEL

Cain and Abel were brothers they
Their story is told unto this day
Abel a righteous man was he
Didn't deserve a brother ugly
Cain was downcast and bi polar
Couldn't get his life in order
Didn't respect the God we know
Nor obedience he did show
Cain killed Abel out of jealousy
The first act of sibling rivalry
Cain did not repent
It was to his detriment
Sibling rivalry at its peak
Abel being a keeper of sheep
Cain a tiller of the land
Presented offering to God by hand
Cain was third cursed by God
First serpent, then ground
Cain went to the land of Nod
God put a mark on him
Gave him grace for his sin


Genesis 4:15 Then the LORD put a mark on Cain to
warn anyone who might try to kill him (NLT)

# COME BEFORE WINTER

Lord, let me seize the day as you told me to do
Let me go forward and always follow through
Using the many gifts that you gave me
Allowing the others always to see
And I always want exactly to be
where and when you place me
to seize each and every opportunity
Seize the day is what you say
Forget about yourself just for today
Doing for others the things that I need
By caring and sharing that's a good deed
Before it's too late I'll do the right thing
Before winter comes and way before spring
I'll look at the way that I'm living today
I'll always be proud and able to say
I was the best that I could be
Always in the company
Of God the Father, Of God the Son
The blessed three all in one
The Holy Spirit by my side
There to lead, there to guide
I won't put off things I know I should do
I won't be a sleeper I care about you!

From Knute Larson's sermon at The Chapel in Akron, Ohio. The second most requested sermon there. First spiritual poetry written.

In winter things die and the purpose of the sermon was to remind us that our life on this earth is short and we need to do things for the Kingdom while we are still here.

Published in Theater of the Mind

# FORGIVE

To forgive is what we need today
Bend your knee and commit to pray
Start afresh to make things new
Renew the right spirit within you
To soar with the eagle on high
All day long and into the "NI"
Forgive and heal your heart and soul
Sent from Him above to us here below
Forgive now and you will see
Just how happy that you can be
The bitterness will melt away
The miracle of God here to stay

Matthew 6:14 if you forgive those who sin against you, your heavenly Father will forgive you. But if you refuse to forgive others, your Father will not forgive your sins. (NLT)

# GRIEF

Death has come into our life
It has affected us so
We're topsey, turvey inside out
We don't know which way to go!
Grief is overwhelming for us to bear
We ponder the whys or where
They are here today and gone tomorrow
Leaving behind overwhelming sorrow
We are selfish at times wanting them to stay
With us on this earth each and every day
Grief never leaves us it only changes
So we can recover and regain our senses
We need a strong FAITH and not question the Lord
They're with Him in heaven, we need to go forward
There is a bigger picture for all of us here
Each life has a plan we need to hold dear
Our citizenship is in heaven, we're in a foreign land
We will see our loved ones again and won't that be grand?


Phil 3:20 But we are citizens of heaven where the Lord Jesus Christ lives and we are eagerly awaiting for him to return as our savior. (NLT)

A citizen is a person who legally belongs to a country and has the rights and protection of that country.

# HEAVEN

Heaven is real I've witnessed that
An angel comes to take us back
To our heavenly home
Where we belong
We're pilgrims on a journey here
Till we get to that place we all hold dear
Was there when dad was walking
Thru the shadow of death
By his side day and night
And in a terrible fright
Wondering when he would go
Then a power to me Jesus did show
It was time and it was so sublime
Jesus waited until I said my last words of love
Then the angel took dad to high above
The peace that I got when the angel took dad
Was awesome and I wasn't sad
At that moment I was very glad
Jesus thought enough of me
To make this power known you see
Heaven is real I've witnessed that!

Luke 16:22 And it came to pass that the beggar died, and was carried by
the angels into Abraham's bosom: the rich man also died, and was buried.
(KJV)

# HOPE

Hope is all that I have for now
Hope always gets me by somehow
When I get up and greet each day
I know that hope is here to stay
Hope is something that you can't loan
You have to keep it and call it your own
Hold on to it both day and night
Even when things are not just right
It's the very best friend that you can have
It's there when you need it and aren't you glad?
Hope is much better than silver or gold
When you are young and when you grow old
Hope is better than fame and fortune you see
I can always be happy and always be
On top of the mountains that come my way
The ones that leave me and the ones that stay
I'm not all alone throughout my life
Through all of my trouble, turmoil, and strife
My friend hope is always there
Hope is all around us everywhere!
The Lord is my hope!


Joel 3:16 but the LORD will be the hope of his people (KJV)

# IT'S YOU LORD

When I get frightened as I sometimes do
It's you Lord you see me through
When I don't like what others say
It's you Lord you brighten my day

When I fall down and I am wrong
It's you Lord you give me a song
When I don't know which way to go
It's you Lord the path you do show

When I get weak and can't go on
It's you Lord you make me strong
When I am hurt and I'm in pain
It's you Lord you stop the rain

When I'm disappointed in what I see
It's you Lord you help me be
The person that you made plans for
It's you Lord that I simply adore!

Jeremiah 29:11 For I know the plans I have for you, says the Lord. They are plans for good and not for disaster, to give you a future and a hope. (NLT)

# I WILL SURVIVE

I will survive this test I've been given
By my Father who is up in heaven
I have His Faith, His Hope, and His Love
They were given to me by Him from above
These fruits I need to survive at best
This life of mine that is ever so blessed
My hopes, my dreams, the goal's I've set
They are waiting for me yet to be met
I will survive this terrible thing
To go on living and being supreme
To give, to share, and to love
All because of Him up above
He is my joy, my strength, my tower
He is more beautiful to me than any flower
So I will just go on with living for now
He'll show me where and show me how
He's still beside me all the while
Going up and down each and every aisle
Every twist and turn and every which way
The bumps in the road both night and day
I will survive this test with flying colors
Because of Him above all the others!

Matthew 28:20 And be sure of this: I am with you always (NLT)

# LOVE IS

Love is not easily offended
Love always was
And always will be
Love is like the eagle
Love has wings
And can soar above
Love has power
Love is stronger than death
And lives on and never dies
Love makes all wrongs right
Overcomes, overlooks
Love is healing and
Never comes too late
Love shines through
Brighter than the sun
Overcome with love
Don't ignore love
We all have sorrows
Look ahead to the tomorrows!

God is Love!


1 John 4:8 But anyone who does not love does not know god – for God is love.

# LOVE NEVER DIES

Love never dies I know to be true
The Lord will see us through
Love thrives on the inside here
When those we hold dear
Go to that heavenly place
For their eternal rest
Death has no power God made it clear
Our love is still here
Hold on to your love and our Father above
Will heal you and set your free
From your grief and misery
Death will come again and again
Learn to trust and turn to Him
Dry those tears and rejoice now
The Lord will show you how!
We need to go on and be strong!

I Corinthians 13:8 Love never dies (The Message Bible)

# MY REASON FOR BEING

I'm here because you blessed me
Why can't the others see?
We are all special to you above
We can all be filled with your love

You created the sun, the moon, the stars
The land, the seas, they are all ours
You made the earth a beautiful place
For each and every one of the human race

You're there, you're here, you're everywhere
Your love, your mercy, your grace to share
To each and every one of us
We all need your special touch
To live our lives and honor you
On this earth and in heaven too!

You've given me your power to do it all
To keep me going so I don't fall
You taught me to be giving and helpful too
You didn't say to only people that I knew

You taught me to be honest so that's what I do
How can I ever really thank you?
To treat people the way that I want to be treated
To be victorious and never be defeated
To forgive those who hurt me
That's why I always want to be

Exactly like you wherever I go
Because I will reap whatever I sow
I will wear a crown one day
If only I would do it your way!


Matthew 6:15 If you forgive those who sin against you, your heavenly Father will forgive you. But if you refuse to forgive others, your Father will not forgive your sins. (NLT)

# RELIGION

Let's not discuss religion
Everyone thinks his own
Is the only way to go
And the way we've all been shown
Is the one true living God
Sitting on his Holy Throne
Jesus the son of God was born
What else do we need to know?
He came to show us the way
How to live day by day
He died for each one of us
So please don't make a fuss
About these man made rules
Saying we have to pay our dues
It's all about faith and nothing else
No matter what they teach
To be a true child of God
Is only to believe
To show love to all
Is our call and not to argue!

Ephesians 2:9 Salvation is not a reward for the good things we have done,
so one of us can boast about it.

# THE LOVE OF GOD

To write about the love of God
There is no way I could
But deep within my very soul
I just feel like I should
The love of God I can't explain
It showers down like rain
How wide, how deep, how long
To make us feel like we belong
He gave His precious son for me
I would never at peace be
To give my only son
For all the world to see
How we are loved by the Lord
How much His love overflows
It fills up our very hearts
Floods us deep within our souls
For us to be transformed like him
Not the way that we've always been

Ephesians 3:18 And may you have the power to understand, as all God's
people should, how wide, how long, how high, and how deep his love
really is. (NLT)

# THE SUNRISE OF OUR TOMORROW

To learn the secret of victorious living
About loving, laughing, and forgiving
Is to trust, obey, and look to the Light
Then weeing may endure only for a night

Tomorrow's sunrise is just a blink away
With hope and joy to start each day
To be able to leap and skip over the hills
Promises that will carry us through life's ills
Today's pain and sorrow will fade away
To the new dawning of a better day
The valleys come and the mountains go
The Light shines through all aglow

No need to be in the valleys for long
He gave us a very special song
Speak to the mountains so they will leave
If only we would just trust and believe
The Way, the Light, our only source
Steering our lives to a better course.

Published in MUSE AND VIEWS – A Kaleidoscope of Poetry,

Published in THE BEST POEMS & POETS OF 2005

John 8:12 Jesus said to the people, "I am the light of the world." (NLT)

# YOUR ADVOCATE

Everyone needs someone to fight for them
Someone who is on their side

When you think you are all alone
Don't be afraid to confide

In your heavenly Father high above
He'll listen, He cares, He's all about love!

# YOUR ADVOCATE

1 John 2:1 My little children I am writing these things to you so that you will not sin. But if anyone does sin, we have an advocate before the Father – Jesus Christ, the Righteous One! (NIV)

# SEASONS

# MARCH MADNESS

My March is between winter and spring
One season ends, the other to begin
On March spring days I wear sunglasses and sing
People wearing shorts have even been seen

On March winter days my boots and I shovel snow
I sit by the fire and drink cocoa!
The March winds continue to blow
Spring's just around the corner
It's time to open the window

In like a lion or out like a lamb?
When the birds come back again
And the smiling sun shining in

Umbrellas, raindrops, sun, and snow
A kaleidoscope of ways to go!


Published in POEMS OF THE WORLD

# SUDDENLY SPRING

March brings the winds
Followed by April showers
Mother Nature's vitamins
For the grass, trees, and flowers
Daylight Savings Time
Shooing away the dark
Anxious for visiting, shopping,
And walking in the park!
The St. Patrick's parties
Signaling the spring
Shamrocks, bow ties and
The wearing of the green
Our earth waking up
Giving us a spring to our step
Looking forward to warmer days
Leaving behind the grayness
I'll open up the windows
And let the fresh air in
I wonder if it's going to snow again?

# MADDENING MAY

Our May was like March this year
Would my herbs die as I did fear?
Sleet, freezing rain, spitting snow
When the harsh winds did blow

We were warned to cover our young seeds
Due to the upcoming freeze
That's what it's like in Ohio
May 16th the wind chill was 20 degrees

I brought my herbs inside
In the warmth they could survive
Will they live or die?
I certainly will try
To revive them again
With soil brought by my friend

I'll cross my fingers and wait
To find out my herbs fate
My basil I love it helps me sleep
My fragrant thyme I want to keep

# SALUTE SEPTEMBER

Summer's end, football games
Followed by October rains

Mums abound, colors of fall
Animals preparing for it all

Memories stored another year
Winter struggles ahead to fear

Cooler mornings, evening breezes
Won't be long everything freezes

Nature falls asleep in part
Another side exposed to art

# FABULOUS FALL

Fall is my favorite time of year
Because I can always hear
The football games with cheering fans
The loud and boisterous high school bands

I love the colorful swaying trees
The cool nights with changing leaves
Fall is my favorite time of year
Because I know the holidays are near

Halloween, Thanksgiving and Christmas too
There will be multitudes of fun things to do
Sharing and caring and giving for all
Thank you Lord for the fall
It is my favorite time of all!

# FAVORING FALL

On our farm we love the fall
Gatherings for one and all
The young, the old and in between
All of them wanting to be seen
To celebrate the summer's end
Waiting for seasons to begin again
We sing, we dance, we clap our hands
Our minds drifting to faraway lands
We roast the bird, we bake the pie
Changes taking place under the sky
The red, the orange, and purple too
Blazing beneath the sky so blue
The landscape with colors so bright
Golden hues throughout the night
The animals seem to know what's in store
Lingering longer behind that barn door
The cool crisp air so clean and fresh
We seem to love the fall the best
Even though it won't be long
We'll be singing a different song
Those faraway lands we'll long to be
Where the sun shines brightly!

(In memory of mom) Published in Poems of Beautiful Ohio – Then and Now

# HAPPY HARVEST

The fall season exciting to me
Holding such a good memory
Pumpkins orange and round
Piles of leaves in a mound
Gourds colorful everywhere
Prize winning going to the fair
Pa working dawn to dusk
Clearing away the corn husk
Corn stalks so straight and tall
Ready to adorn our harvest wall
Wagons full of apples picked by hand
Growing everywhere on our land
Ma in her kitchen cooking with care
Golden locks, fallen wisps of hair
The pumpkin pies to me were the best
Pa liked the minced meat above the rest
Our little house in the country
Was aglow with all the bounty
Neighbors came from afar and shared
Playing the fiddle and they all cared
(In memory of mom)


Published in Poems of Beautiful Ohio – Then and Now

Published in Famous Poets of the Heartland

# THE TREES

The trees are bare
They have no care
The leaves have gone, but where?
I can imagine, but do I dare?
Did they feel any pain
From all that rain?
That drove them to the ground
Final phase blowing all around
Bare trees have a personality
Twisted branches a finality
Their beauty stolen from them
With time it's restored again
The bud on a branch unlike a newborn
Looks to be ever so forlorn
It's tiny and sturdy to be
I wait and I watch till I see
The bud is first then comes the leaf
At last I can sigh with relief
For then I know it won't be long
Till the days are lighter, the birds sing their song
All of our lives resemble a leaf
We're here and then our life all too brief!

James 4:14 For your life is like the morning fog it's here a little while, then it's gone. (NLT)

# NOTORIOUS NOVEMBER

November with its ups and downs
It's always a guessing game
Should I go or should I stay?
They are calling for rain
The temperature will drop rapidly
All the way down to twenty
Then the ice followed by snow
I had many places to go
The leaves are falling right along with the snow
They're confused and don't know which way to go!
I'm sweeping the leaves and shoveling the snow
Nature surprised us and put on quite a show
I need to prepare for the following days
This season will bring me I'll have to change my ways
Everyone else right along with me
I will have lots of company
Next week it will be up to seventy
Then we'll be getting ready for the turkey
Winter coat, summer jacket, or sweater to wear?
We'll be happy and celebrate and won't really care!

# SPARKLING SNOW

Sparkling snow all around
It glistens and glitters in the sunlight
Like diamonds
Falling to the ground
Covering the hillside like a blanket
Draping the branches of the trees
Like cotton candy
The beauty is everywhere
Painting the landscape in white
Suddenly changes begin to take place
a down pour of snow like rain
Piling up on streets, in driveways,
On sidewalks
Schools closed, meetings cancelled
Traffic accidents, lives lost
Danger
A loss of beauty
White snow turns to gray snow then black like coal
Stone cold snow then ice
Snow melts, floods
More lives lost
More danger
The sparkling snow is no more

# STORMS

Storms are severe
This time of year
I pray they don't come near
Homes have been lost
Including life
I pray those survive
What will they do?
Only God can see them thru
To start anew
The tornadoes touch down
Toss everything around
It seems they're longer
On the ground as long as an hour
I saw in one state
I don't know their exact fate
The roads washed away by all that rain
It came down again and again
People stranded in those trees
Tornadoes and flooding stop please!

Published in POEMS OF THE WORLD

# WHERE DID WINTER GO THIS YEAR?

Where did winter go?
Warmer temps she did show
No ice or snow!
No snow blowers or shovels today
Kids outside playing like in May
Wardrobes different for this season
No one seems to know the reason
Spring and summer temps
Setting records, Goodyear blimps
Up in the air we see
So plain and clearly
Unusual for this time of year
Especially in Ohio here
Don't put your shovels away
Spring in February isn't here to stay
Winter hasn't gone to bed
He will rear his ugly head
Six days before spring
A snow storm winter did bring

# DAYS OF REMEMBERANCE

# THE SHAMROCK

The shamrock resembles the shape of the cross
So St. Patrick could save all of the lost!
God the Father, God the Son,
God the Holy Spirit all in one
To teach them about His Son!

Our Father had that in mind all along
To bring Ireland to His Son
St. Patrick answered that call,
Went back to save one and all!
Wat a great thing St. Patrick did
And all honor him even when
They're not Irish nor Catholic be
St. Patrick changed history!
Some wear green and drink green beer
I will always hold St. Patrick dear!
Let's celebrate him this year!

# HAPPY ST. PATRICK'S DAY

# MY HALLOWEEN OF YESTERDAY

My Halloween of yesterday doesn't seem that far away
The fun we had cannot be duplicated to this day

My costumes weren't that great or fine
They were acceptable because they were mine
I didn't have an orange decorated bag
Just the brown paper one that I had to lag
That came from the grocery store
I carried it from door to door

At times I carried the pillow case
Brown paper bag was lost in haste
The ghosts, the goblins, the supermen
No need to fear way back then
It was a different day
No pins in apples, no razor blades
Couldn't be any other way

Some candy unwrapped and loose as could be
My mother didn't have a care and neither me
The doctor's house I never passed
He always gave the best
A standard sized candy bar
Rated high above the rest

I could go alone on those very streets
That I ran and played until dusk
Walk slow or fast or run
There was no need to rush

Never ate my loot along the way
Wanted to hurry home and stay
Had to find a hiding place
To keep my candy safe
Except from dad above the rest
I saved for him the best!

# MY HALLOWEEN OF YESTERDAY!

# ALL SAINT'S DAY

Death now has no power
We are delivered that hour
All Saint's Day was meant to be
Honoring those living eternally

Darkness now rules that day
The grave stones, skeletons
Paving the way
World's way of honoring the dead
Scary by witches and goblins led

Death has no sting
So don't be afraid
The Light is still shining bright
Jesus has come to our aid!


I Corinthians 15: 54,55 Death is swallowed up in victory. O death, where is your victory! O death, where is your sting?" (NLT)

# THANKFUL THANKSGIVING

I always made the pumpkin pies
The turkey and the dressing
Thanksgiving to us was a huge blessing
Dad came the night before
Always knocking at my door
Being all alone that night
He always made it just right
He came for the pumpkin pies
To me it was no surprise
I could always count on him
To be here that special night
Mr. "Blue Eyes" shining bright!
I did make extra pies for him
Was the least that I could do
My memories of him that night
Are always shining through
His big smile and stories unfold
To brighten up my life
I miss that man so much it hurts
He was my special sun burst


I thank God for the Christian dad that I had!

I Thessalonians 5:18 In everything give thanks (NLT)

# JESUS

# FRUITFUL FORGIVENESS

"Go and sin no more"
Jesus said

"Father forgive them"
As He bled
On the cross that
Mournful day

He came and taught us
How to pray

A baby born to die for all
He died because of Adam's fall

Trust and obey
There's a better way

Confess the sin
Be with Him again!


Luke 23:34 Jesus said "Father, forgive them, for they don't know what they are doing." And the soldiers gambled for his clothes throwing dice. (NLT)

# HIGH PRIEST

On the cross where Jesus died
Two criminals hung by his side
He was innocent, but yet was tried
They called it crucified
Jesus suffered and died on that cross
For our blessings and all of the lost
What a huge cost the price He paid
In a borrowed tomb He was laid
He came back to life in three days
And to him we owe our praise
Jesus is our High Priest indeed
Because of Him we have been freed
We can go directly to our Father above
Whose Holy Spirit came down like a dove
Jesus continues to pray for us all
He lifts us up when we do fall
Our problems are always on His mind
Because of His love and He is so kind
Jesus we thank you!
Without you Jesus what would we do?


Published in Voices in Verse – Weaving Words

Hebrews 4:14 Therefore, since we have a great high priest who has ascended into heaven, Jesus the son of God, let us hold firmly to the faith we profess (NIV)

# JESUS

Jesus is gentle and humble in heart
The people tried to tear him apart
The same ones who shouted "Hosanna" that way
Were screaming out loud "Crucify him today"
Jesus told his friends he wouldn't be with them
How could this be? They said they loved him!
They didn't want him to die and fade away
But in that tomb he did lay
He had to be scourged and put to rest
To fulfill his destiny and pass that test
Of the prophecies that were foretold
By so many of those prophets of old
After three days he was alive
Resurrected, and perfect, to survive
Thru him we can have rest for our soul
Not just above, but down here below
No other means of escape that we know
He taught us the way to go!

John 12:13 They took palm branches and went out to meet him shouting "Hosanna!! Luke 23:21 But they kept shouting "Crucify him!" "Crucify him!" (NIV)

# JESUS IS MY TRUE NORTH

Jesus is my True North
I follow him every day
As I read my Bible and pray

His power to me He does show
It's all about Him I know!
He is with me day and night
He's able to make thing just right!

I want my steps to be ordered by Him
That's the way it's always been
To please Him in every way
His praises I continually say!

## JESUS IS MY TRUE NORTH

To find your true North is to get on the right course. True North is your orienting point – your fixed point in a spinning world that helps you stay on track. It is your internal compass representing who you are at your deepest level!

4/30/17 prior to Sunday Service at Lighthouse Church

# JESUS' LOVE

Jesus beaten, bleeding,
Hanging on that cross
Bearing the sins
For all of the lost

Struggling for breath
He could not even rest
Thoughts on his mother
With love
That pure, deep kind
Sent from above

Jesus said:
"John, my beloved,
Take care of her
She is your mother now"
"Mother, John will be your son
Soon, before this day is done"

John 19:27 and to the disciple, "Here is your mother." From that time on, this disciple took her into his home. (NIV)

# JESUS' POWER

I've learned to trust in Jesus power
Day by day and hour by hour
I've learned to trust in Jesus' name
I will never be the same
Hour by hour and minute by minute
I know that Jesus is always in it
I need your grace every day
Lord please help me as I pray
Help me to do what you called me
Let your presence always be
Where I am every minute every hour
Show me, show me, Lord your power
Lord, O Lord, I love you so
Help me, help me as I go
Day by day and week by week
Oh help me Lord as I seek
Lord I praise you here and now
Show me where Lord show me how
I've learn to trust in Jesus' power
Lord, Oh hear me in this hour!

Acts 10:38 How God anointed Jesus of Nazareth
with the Holy Spirit and with power. (ESV)

# MY SON SHINE

You light up the sky so bright
You light up my life so right!

You make things shine!

The dew on the grass, the trees so bare
The flowers you care, even the birds in the air

You make things grow!

My spirit overflowing with your love
My peace, my comfort sent from above

You bring much joy!

You comfort me when things go wrong
You give me hope so I can go on!

You are light and life!
Darkness can never extinguish it!


John 1:4 Life itself was in him, and this life gives light
to everyone. The light shines through the darkness and
the darkness can never extinguish it. (NLT)

# MY REDEEMER

Jesus came from heaven to earth
Brought forth by a virgin birth
He came to show me the way
What a price he had to pay

I want to honor him in all ways
While here the rest of my days
I do think of him every day
It isn't enough just to pray

To read my Bible and learn of him
That's the way it's always been
I would like to show him more
The way to heaven, he is the door

I'm so thankful for what he did
Washed away all of my sin
Thank you is such a small word for him
I'll be grateful to the end!


John 10:9 I am the door: by me if any man enter in, he shall be saved, and shall go in and out, and find pasture. (KJV)

# OUR SAVIOR

Jesus Christ was born that day
Laid in a manger covered in hay
In wisdom he did grow
He showed us the way to go

He was all about power
Preparing for that final hour

He was mocked and betrayed
He was put to shame
But there is no greater name
He will always reign!

Nothing can produce the joy he can give
The straight and narrow way to live


Luke 2:52 And Jesus grew in wisdom and stature, and in favor with God and man. (NIV)

# CHRISTMAS

# A CHRISTMAS MIRACLE

A Christmas miracle on that day
So long ago and far away

To save us all from our sins
One life ends, the other begins

Made possible thru his birth
Our heavenly Father came down to earth

To show his love for all to see
What more could he do for you and me?


John 1:1 In the beginning the Word already existed. He was with God, and he was God. John 1:14 So the Word became human and lived here on earth among us. He was full of unfailing love and faithfulness. (NLT)

# CHERISH CHRISTMAS

Christmas shines all around me
All year long
Not just today in all ways
Born far away

The love and light of Jesus Christ
Is where I belong
His light ever glowing

Forever it's showing
His grace and truth for all
Especially when we fall
He is the reason for the season

Not the gifts, the cookies,
The parties at best
He is way above all the rest

Happy Birthday King Jesus!


John 1:5 The light shines through the darkness, and the darkness can never extinguish it. (NLT)

# CHRISTMAS DAY

Long ago and far away
A child was born on Christmas Day
In a town called Bethlehem
There was no room in the inn
In a manger surrounded by hay
Was where the baby had to lay

This child was God come down to earth
That is why we celebrate his birth
He was named Jesus and brought us joy
Wrapped in a cloth the baby boy
Lived not a mansion or a palace
This Holy King lived right among us!

Luke 2:7 She gave birth to her first child, a son. She wrapped him snugly in strips of cloth and laid him in a manger, because there was no room for them in the village inn. (NLT)

# CHRISTMAS (JESUS)

Christmas (Jesus) makes the world a better place
For you and me, the whole human race
The merriment in every home
Rejoicing, laughing, singing along

Special services honoring the story of old
That joyous day above all others
Peace for all of our sisters and brothers

The precious light who was born that day
Guiding and leading us along our way
Making life bearable and full of hope
The life he gives allowing to cope

Come what may and it will come
But we won't be all alone!


Hebrews 13:5 "I will never fail you. I will never forsake you." (NLT)

Published in POEMS OF THE WORLD

# CHRISTMAS SEASON

The season of love
Sent down from above
That holy night so long ago

God's special gift
In a baby boy
So full of peace and joy

The light of the night
Shining so bright

That small babe
In a manger was laid

For all to know
Down here below

The way, the truth, the life
So we don't lose sight!


John 14:6 Jesus told them: "I am the way, the truth, and the life. No one can come to the Father except through me." (NLT)

# CHRISTMAS STAR

Our Christmas Star
So high, so bright
Shining throughout the night

To announce the birth
Of our Holy King
Everywhere it could be seen

By the shepherds in the fields
And to the Magi from afar
Traveling two years later
Under that same star
How long on earth did it beam?
That glorious awesome thing

Our Christmas Star
So high, so bright
Shining throughout the night!


Matthew 2:2 Where is the newborn king of the Jews? We have seen his star as it arose, and we have come to worship him." (NLT)

Published in POEMS OF THE WORLD

# GLORY IN THE HIGHEST

While shepherds watched their flocks by night
They beheld the most wonderful sight
An angel of the Lord appeared there
And glory in the highest was everywhere
They were greatly afraid to behold this sight
The angel assured them things would be all right

The angel brought tidings of great joy
That came to earth that night in a boy
Born in the city of David a savior
Wrapped in swaddling cloths in a manger
There was a multitude of heavenly hosts
Praising our God in heaven to the utmost

The angels went back to heaven that night
The shepherds had gotten over their fright
They went to Bethlehem to find their savior
They did find him lying in a manger
It was then that the shepherds returned
Praising God for the things they had learned

Luke 2:8 That night some shepherds were in the fields outside the village, guarding their flocks of sheep. Suddenly, an angel of the Lord appeared among them, and the radiance of the Lord's glory surrounded them. They were terribly frightened. (NLT)

# JESUS BORN TO DIE

Jesus was born to die
No need to ask me why

Realizing makes me sigh
At times I even cry

He came for you and me
For the whole world to see

His birth, his pain, his sorrow
To help us meet our tomorrow!

Isaiah 53:3 He was despised and rejected – a man of sorrows acquainted
with bitterest grief.

# THE CHRISTSMAS GIFT

Christ the King was born one day
The angels sang and also did say
"Do not be afraid for we bring great joy"
Christ the king came down as a boy
To change the whole world for the better
For each man and woman down to the letter
He brought with him love, joy, and peace
Nothing compares and will never cease
With what he did for us forevermore
Everything he had he did outpour
He died on a cross for you and me
Hue suffered and the people of old did see
He was brave and slaughtered as a lamb
He was sent down from the great "IAM"
How small and shallow we feel inside
Not measuring up because he died
For all of us great and small every where
He gave us everything because of his care
We can thank God for his mercy and love
For sending us this worthy gift from above

Published on a Christmas card

Published in Timeless Voices

# THE MAGIC OF CHRISTMAS

The magic of Christmas is in the air
I can see and feel it everywhere
The Christmas tree lights so colorful and bright
Lighting up homes all through the night
The shops overflowing with customers galore
Frantically racing from store to store
Searching laboriously for just the right thing
For her, for him, all happiness to bring
The cookies, the candy, the greetings abound
Smiles, laughter, joyous gifts to be found
Green, red, gold, and blue
The colors of Christmas all around you
Let's not forget the reason for the season
There are those who do
But that's not for me and you
Christ the King came down that day
A baby born among straw and hay
To save us all from our sins
He wipes the slate clean to begin again
Thank God for the greatest gift of all
The magic of Christmas is in Him!

Published in POEMS OF THE WORLD

# THE SPIRIT OF CHRISTMAS

The Spirit of Christmas sent from above
To us down here filled with love
The way, the life, the truth he gave
To fellow men for us he saved

That day so blessed forevermore
His way and his life we do adore
He brought down with him
Peace and joy within

He will live eternally
And so will we
If only we would just
Trust and believe!

# THE SPIRIT OF CHRISTMAS

November 15, 2015, at The Chapel in Akron, Ohio, during Sunday service

Published in POEMS OF THE WORLD

# OUR HEAVENLY FATHER

# GOD

Our Father in the heavens
Our savior
Our teacher
Our provider

Our protector
Our healer
Our shepherd
Our present help
In time of trouble

Our blessing
Our saving grace
Our tender mercies
So full of love, our Father!

I John 3:1 See how much our heavenly Father loves us, for he allows us to be called his children, and we really are! But the people who belong to this world don't know God, so they don't understand that we are his children. (NLT)

I John 4:16 God is love, and all who live in love live in God, and God lives in them. (NLT)

# GOD'S CREATION

The beauty of God's creation amazes me
It is something grand to see
The trees, the flowers, the sky, the water
Who do some think that it is a bother?
To thank God for each and every day
To thank him for guiding and protecting their way
To praise his wonderful blessed name
He always loves us just the same
Whether we know him or praise him not
He is there for all not to be forgot
He deserves the best that we can give
Whether we're spotless or in our sin
He accepts us right where we are
All of us from near and from far
We only have to kneel and say
"I've sinned Lord forgive me today
Show me the way that I should go
I will try not to hurry and take it slow"

Psalm 19:1 The heavens tell of the glory of God. The skies display his marvelous craftsmanship! (NLT)

Psalm 27:11 Teach me how to live, O LORD. Lead me along the path of honestly, for my enemies are waiting for me to fall! (NLT)

# GOD WATCHES US

God loves us each and every one
Before noon and after the sun
Goes down each and every day
While we work or while we play

He sends his angels to keep us safe
Each and every single place
That we will be day or night
He loves us with all his might

We can't escape his watchful eye
So why do we always try
To be and do what we always want
Instead of the things that we should not?
Just to be where he places me
Is exactly where I want to be!


Proverbs 15:3 The LORD is watching everywhere, keeping his eye on both the evil and the good (NLT)

# HIS LOVE

Nurture his love and it will grow
Diminishing darkness it will glow
A gift from God to overcome
So that we are not overrun
With our hurt, our pain, our grief
He's given his love for our relief
His unfailing love protects all around
It's strong, t's sincere, and oh so sound
With his love comes joy and peace
Allowing bitterness to be released
His love heals all wounds and pride
Completeness needed to abide
Beside our Shepherd every day
His love guiding us all the way
His promise of reward will be great
When we reach that pearly gate

Psalm 118:1 Give thanks to the LORD, for he is good! His faithful love endures forever. (NLT)

Published in OUR 100 FAMOUS POETS by Famous Poets

# IS GOD REAL?

The sun, the moon, the stars above
Are testament of his overflowing love
What else could he possibly do
To prove his very existence to you?
"There is no God" a fool will say
Then who created night and day?
The seas, the animals, plant and trees
Last, but not least you and me
He branded within us his very mark
The knowledge of right and wrong
The way for us to be strong
How to endure and for how long
A path to perfect peace all of our days
If only we would just stop and pray
Bend your knee and rest quietly
Allow your soul to find peace and safety

Genesis 1:1 In the beginning God created the heavens and the earth. Psalm 14:1 Only fools say in their hearts, "There is no God." Ephesians 1:13 And when you believed in Christ, he identified you as his own by giving you the Holy Spirit, whom he promised long ago. Philippians 4:13 For I can do everything with the help of Christ who gives me the strength I need. (NLT)

# OUR HIDING PLACE

We can go to our father and hide anytime
He's our refuge, our strength to abide
He will always be our High Tower
In him indwells all power

He has proved his faithfulness
And we have truly been blessed
In times of trouble he's always there
Surrounding us and showing his care

There is no need for us to fear
He said he would dry our every tear
If the mountains crumble into the sea
He's still our refuge, our strength to be

Now and forever more!


Psalm 46:1 -3 God is our refuge and strength, always ready to help in times of trouble. So we will not fear, even if earthquakes come and the mountains crumble into the sea. Let the oceans roar and form. Let the mountains tremble as the waters surge! (NLT)

# YOU ARE

You are a beacon of hope
An anchor of faith

Our abiding shadow
A shelter and fortress

Our dwelling place

We are storm tossed
Helpless and lost

You bring us
to a safe harbor

Psalm 91:1 Those who live in the shelter of the Most High will find rest in the shadow of the Almighty.

Psalm 91:2 This I declare of the LORD: He alone is my refuge; my place of safety; he is my God, and I am trusting him. (NLT)

# PATRIOTIC

# AMERICA STRONG

AMERICA STRONG
That's who we are
With God behind us
We can go far
Are we on a slippery slope?
If so, God is our only hope
It's all about wanting to pray
So our father in heaven will show us the way
We will be safe once more
Only when our God rules
In government, our homes, our schools
We've all turned away from him
Let's go back to that Rock again
Put him back where he belongs
So we can be AMERICA STRONG!

# AN AMERICAN HERO

Chris Kyle my hero above all the rest
They say he was the very best
He saved so many of our men

He went back to fight again and again
To a terrible war zone
When he could have been home
Then his life came to an abrupt end

He was killed by one of his own
A patriotic man in that heavenly place
God giving him a much deserved rest
To honor this man and what he did

His gifts he shared so many could live
A family man, an American sniper, a Navy Seal
This talented man of God was oh so real
Chris Kyle
MY AMERICAN HERO

Published in MUSE AND VIEWS – A Kaleidoscope of Poetry

# A SON OF FREEDOM

For freedom he will stand and fight

Kiss me goodbye and leave my sight

Maybe forever not to come home

I pray not to be left alone

He's A SON OF FREEDOM

My hero, my man!

Loves the Red, White, and Blue

Through and through

So thankful that he loves me too!

## A SON OF FREEDOM

# LET FREEDOM RING!

Mountain tops to sea shores
School yards to college dorms
Toddler to senior
Heavier to leaner
Student to teacher
Congregation to preacher
LET FREEDOM RING!
Store fronts to home fronts
Bustling crowds to lonely hearts
Battlefield to White House steps
Households to State Reps
La Nina to El Nino
Raindrops to falling snow
LET FREEDOM RING!
Heaven above
Cascading below
LET FREEDOM RING!
For all to know!

Published in AMERICA – "Let Freedom Reign" – OUR SACRIFICES – OUR HEROES

Published in Famous Poets of the Heartland

# MIRACLE ON THE HUDSON RIVER

The miracle on the Hudson River
It happened with such great speed
So many heroes serving and helping
And doing their good deed

They quickly reacted
and moved with great haste
For many there wasn't
a single moment to waste

The biggest hero the pilot
Who saved so many lives
Not slighting the policemen
Performing all those dives

Made sure the last survivor
Was out of harm's way
There was just enough time
They knew they couldn't stay
Inside that wrecked plane
That was already sinking
They had to hurry and get out
Was exactly what they were thinking
The passengers all heard the prayers being said
They were rising up to heaven way above their heads
Our Heavenly Father above came to their rescue
He quickly reacted and did what no one else could do

He guided Sully's thoughts, his maneuvers, and his hand
Steering his course to that magnificent safe land!


Published in AMERICA – "Let Freedom Reign" OUR SACRIFICES –
OUR HEROES"

Published in POEMS OF THE WORLD

# MY COUNTRY

The United States of America is the best place to be
It's the home of the brave and the land of the free!
We have freedom of speech and security too
It's the best place to be and I hope that you

Will take advantage of each and every day
Whether at school or work or play
To be the best that you can be
For all the other countries to see
We have high morals and character too
And try to show it in everything we do
We honor God in all of His glory
He will honor us if we do and that is the story

We pray for our President, our military too
All heroes who fight fire and policemen in blue
Our doctors, our nurses, our teachers wherever
We pray and ask God to make things better

For us and our future whatever to hold
The land of the FREE and the home of the BOLD

This country was founded on Godly principals you see
And that is the reason that we can be FREE
To choose our president, the church of our choice
To work, to play and to have a voice
The United States of America is where I want to be
The home of the brave and the land of the free!


Published in Today's Famous Poems, On the Wings of Pegasus

Published in AMERICA – "Let Freedom Reign" OUR SACRIFICES –
OUR HEROES

# OUR LIBERTY!

Climb to the top and stay there
Liberate and be carefree
Let the masses see that you can be
Who you were meant to be
It is embedded in our soul and spirit
Our climbing freedom
The oxygen we breathe

OUR LIBERTY!

Liberty, we are destined to be free
Our liberty to know and to think
To move and to be creative
Give us our liberty at the high cost
That was paid for by so many
Our happiness, our peace, our life

OUR LIBERTY!

Thank God for our founders and our liberty
And our destiny in Him
Don't limit our liberty
And don't try to extinguish it
Deposit liberty in our lives
Liberty to do what we want
And liberty to do what we ought

There's no liberty in wrong doing
Be liberated to do the right thing
Let liberty ring for all like a loud bell!

OUR LIBERTY!


Published in AMERICA – "Let Freedom Reign" – OUR SACRIFICES –
OUR HEROES

# RED, WHITE, & BLUE

Red, White, and Blue
Our flag so free
Courage and bravery!

Strength unfold
Ever so bold

RED, WHITE & BLUE
Ever so true!

# THE SONS OF FREEDOM

The red, white and blue

I'll always be true

The sons who fight for me and you

In the cold thru the storms

Leave their kids and warm homes

They go into the night

For our freedom to fight

Kiss their loved ones goodbye

So our freedom won't die

The sons of freedom born to be

The sons who fight for you and me!

# THE UNITED STATES MILITARY

The Unites States Military how great that they are!
They come from all over from near and from far
All the branches band together in unity
It's a grand thing for the whole world to see
They so without sleep and they care so much
They affect everything they see and touch
They're brave, courageous, and honorable too
They fight for freedom for me and for you
They leave their homes and families alone
To protect us and we need to condone
What they stand for and wherever they go
We need to praise them and always show
Our support for them in bad times and in good
And each and every one of us should
Be proud of our military regardless of who
Because they support the red, white, and blue
They fight the storms and where the winds blow
Their wisdom and their power they do show
The United States Military is a force to behold
They are the best that there is and ever so bold
I thank my God in the heavens above
For the United States Military and their love!


Published in AMERICA "Let Freedom Reign" – OUR SACRIFICES –
OUR HEROES

# HUMOR

# AN UNFORTUNATE YEAR

January was here
First month of the year
Hurt my knees doing yoga
The pain was severe
Easter the sump pump was on the fritz
Naturally it couldn't be fixed
Summer came and the stove acted up
My car was totaled by a Fed Ex truck

My new security system wouldn't back track
And, of course, it had to be sent back!
The furnace was replaced in the fall
Most expensive purchase of them all
Except for the car that I bought on credit
So far: sump pump, stove, car, furnace,
Security system, how can I forget it?

Christmas came and the washer was leaking
Instead of buying gifts a washer I was seeking
Christmas day evening the faucets were bad
New faucets by family
My brother in law is handy!

A new year came
Thank God for my kin
It's starting all over again
Here comes the snow
The snow blower won't go!
There is no end!

I am so blessed so I'll give it a rest
Thank you Geoff Melucci you are the best!

Published in POEMS OF THE WORLD

# MY FRACTURED TOE

I broke my toe
No place to go
Stayed home from church
It really hurts!
Home all alone
Nursing my pain
Hoping to regain
My strength again
To go out and come in!

Went to the mall to get flats one day
Had to go to bed right away
Walking on that toe was too much for me
It throbbed for days and even hurt my knee!
Limping is so detrimental for me to do
I'll just show my toes in Sunday School!
Open-toed sandals will have to do!
It's been weeks now limping in pain
My strength I just want to regain
No more walking barefoot in the house is my aim!

# MY NEIGHBORS

They always want favors – MY NEIGHBORS
I have to forgive and forget
Whenever they're mad and they fret
I babysit and spend my time
Trying to keep their kids in line
I do this for free
They take advantage of me
I have to keep peace with – MY NEIGHBORS

Their kids are in my house all summer
And it's getting to be such a bummer!
I've spent all my money on them
I wonder and question just when
They will do a favor for me
For I live all alone you see
I have to keep peace with – MY NEIGHBORS

Their cats are supposed to be kept
Inside their house as a pet
I've tried the moth balls to kill
Their odor and it's unpleasant still
I have to keep peace with –MY NEIGHBORS

Published in Lucidity Journal

# THE BIG SALE

First day of the sale
I've got to get going
I'm debating on it
Because it is snowing
I've waited all week
For this day
Should I go or should I stay?
My heart's desire
Is to beat the rush
Don't even care if the
Snow turns to mush!
I get bundled up
As snug as a bug
And on my way out
I tripped on the rug
My body is bruised
With so many aches
Why didn't I
Just put on the brakes?
Now I sit all alone
Stuck in my home
I missed the big sale
There will be another one!

# ROMANCE

# ARE YOU THE ONE?

I wonder if you're the one for me
At times it is difficult to see
Because of what I am feeling now
I need to know if it's real somehow
You came along at just the right time
But will you really always be mine?
You seem to be the one for me
Bur can it really somehow be
The one I've waited for all of my life
To live with you forever and be your wife?
You always say the right thing to me
You're exactly where I want you to be
By my side both night and day
Is where I always want you to stay!

# FROZEN IN TIME

We're frozen in time
You call to me
I can't answer you

You promise me a tower
I decline your proposal

You give me undying love
All I can give is friendship

You grace my life with gifts
I can't offer you anything

You pave my way with greatness
I can't follow you!

We're frozen in time!

# KEEP THE PORCH LIGHT ON

New beginnings
Excitement around the corner
Help is on the way
Expand your horizons

Jump start your hope
Ignite that fire
Clear the cobwebs

# KEEP THE PORCH LIGHT ON

# OUR DECLARATION OF LOVE

Today is the day that we declare our love
To everyone here and to our Father above
To care, to share, to love, to give
To each other and even when

The dark clouds come, the sun will rise
When we look into each other's eyes
And see the love, the caring ways
That will keep us together all of our days

Beside each other both night and day
Is exactly where we should always stay
To comfort each other when we are down
With God we can turn anything around

We've waited for this our whole life
To live, to love as husband and wife
And so today on this our wedding day
We pray for God's blessings along our way!


For Wedding Vows

Written and recited during lighting of candles during friend's wedding

Published in SONGS OF HONOUR

# TO MY LOVE

You're my hero, you're my friend
So in love I've never been
You're there for me when I am down
You can turn anything around

You lift me up when I am blue
I'm so happy that you are true
You are the wind beneath my wings
To me you will always be all things

You always say the right thing to me
You're exactly where I want you to be
By my side both night and day
Is where I want you always to stay

You inspire me to be
All that I was meant you see
I've waited for you all of my life
To live, to love, to be your wife
And so today on this our wedding day
I wish you health, wealth, and happiness
Along our way!

Written for Wedding Vows

# TWILIGHT TO DAWN

Twilight to dawn
Oh how I long
To have you in my sight
All through the night
So far and yet near
You'll always be dear
Just like the stars above
I am that sure of my love
There's never a doubt within me
I don't know how to make you see
You question my integrity
I know we were meant to be
Give me the time
And you will be mine
Thru all eternity!

# TRIBUTES

# IN MEMORY OF DAD

I've written this poem in memory of you
For me and all of your loved ones too!
You were the best that you could be
Those around you could always see
Your loving, caring, and giving ways
I try to remember all of your days
No one has ever impressed me so much
I will never forget your very special touch
You were brave, strong, and gentle too
No one else that I see compares to you
I learned so much from what you did and said
As time goes by I will always be led
By your high morals and character too
Each and every day I try to do
What you taught me by action and deed
It's everything that I will ever need
To get me through this life of mine
My only dream is that I will shine
Like you did when you were here too
I want to be exactly like you!

Published on poetry.com

# MY TREASURE

He was my treasure
My silver, my gold, my jewel
His smile lit up the room
His laughter warmed me

His love was tangible
It surrounded me
He told me I could never do anything
To destroy his love for me

He raised me, he adored me
He supported me in
Everything I did
He protected me
He never criticized me
I miss you dad!

# A TRIBUTE TO DAD

I've written this especially for you
For your birthday and all of us too!
In your lifetime I'm sure you have seen it all
Thru all the seasons: summer, winter, spring and fall

That day was special your date of birth
You were born to James and Velma on this earth
You did have five sisters and four brothers
They were special to you and there were no others
Mary, Jean, Kathryn, Florence and Violet were the girls
They were mostly brunettes and one was blonde with curls

John, Don, Tony, and Bill were the boys
You didn't have much money nor had many toys
You gave some of them nicknames it's true
Pipe, Ape, Crip, Blackie, Baby, and
They gave a special one to you
The nickname that they gave you was Frost
I think it's because you were always the boss!
Your worked hard and helped support your family
It was a grand thing for everyone to see!
You left your family and came to Akron to work
You met our mother and fell in love that was the perk!
You had a wonderful life with her it's true
And we all loved her as much as you

You and mom had two girls and two boys
We brought you many heartaches and many joys
Carolyn was born to you and mom first
And we all know that you could just burst
With happiness, pride and caring too
Jim, Tom, and I were born to you!

153

Carolyn and I were just like twins
Along comes Jim and the fun begins
Tom was the baby and he was born last
He was a joy to all, I remember the past

Carolyn, Jim, Tom, and I are now your treasures
We like to think that we bring you pleasures
We know that you love us very much
Because you are concerned, you worry, and such

We've given you nine grandchildren to fill your days
They are all unique and different in their ways
Hal was born first then came Jay, Jimbo, Brian, and Brandi
Tom gave us Sammy, Andy, Sarah, and little Sadie who likes candy
Even though you don't know it you've accomplished so much
You've given us all your very special touch
And so today on your birthday
We wish you love, health, and happiness
the rest of your way!

Rev.

Published by International Library of Poetry, ON GOSSAMER WINGS, and on CD that went around the world by them with other poets by a professional reader

# THREE RED ROSES

(In memory of my sister Carolyn)
Three red roses I had put in your bouquet
When you were in Hospice that day
And by your side they would stay
One represented our mom
To heaven she has gone
One represented you
My sister of true blue

Lastly the one represented me
I was there for everyone to see
The three musketeers throughout our days
All that time just seemed to slip away

Then you were gone to up above
Another bouquet of flowers including
three red roses to show my love
Today for your memorial alone am I
looking up into the blue, blue sky
I have my three red roses with me
The three of us forever to be
Always in my memory!

# FORGIVENESS

(In memory of my brother)

I forgive you for hurting me
I forgive you for failing to see
That I loved you with all my heart
You allowed things to tear us apart
I'll never know what you wouldn't forgive
All those years and now I live
Without your voice, your face, your laugh
To think that I was always last
If you only knew the love I had
It was so good and never bad
I helped raise you when you were a boy
To all of us you were a joy!
I want to remember a happy day
Before you left and went away
Maybe we could have been best friends
I regret to say this story ends
Didn't you know how I would cry?
I was denied my final goodbye
Because you wouldn't forgive
And I always thought you were my friend

# LOVE AKRON

Love Akron was founded by Pastor Ford
A man by many who is so adored
He prayed, he struggled for all to see
just trying to bring about unity
to Akron, Ohio, with its ups and downs
he prayed to turn wrong things around
With God behind him all the way
he can teach you how to pray
This pastor is a praying man
With you he will always stand
For what is right, for what is true
He honors the red, white, and blue
His love for Akron is evident
Trying to birth love is prevalent
His main job and goal to achieve
We need to trust him and believe
For what he stands for and is trying to do
About the betterment for me and for you
It's been in his mind for decades now
to turn Akron, Ohio, around some how
So please stand with him in solidarity
It will be a grand thing and not just for clergy!

# ITALIANS

# LINDA LAURENTI MILLER

Linda Miller a friend she has been
She will be here to the end
Met my dad at church before me
My best friend is she
We worked at the same company
She was the first to hold my baby
She stood with me when dad died
at the hospital by my side
day and night, night and day
she stayed and didn't go away
That meant so very much
I won't forget her special touch
She supported me through the years:
The laughter, the heart ache, and the tears
We went to the same church for years
When I'm upset she doesn't fret
Full of wisdom she does get
So today Linda I honor you
To thank you for all that you do!
HAPPY BIRTHDAY!

# CARMAN LICCIARDELLO AND DAD

Carman Licciardello you're the MAN
Dad was your biggest FAN
Not just because you are Itali-AN
Two Italian Stallions on a FIGHT
To save everyone in their SIGHT!
Italians bring so much to our COUNTRY
Talented men of God so blessed to BE
St. Patrick saved a whole COUNTRY
He was Italian you SEE
So please don't argue with ME
Michelangelo such a talented MAN
Blessed us with beauty by God's HAND
Italians everywhere in our LAND
Now they claim Shakespeare was Itali-AN
Christopher Columbus, Leonardo da Vinci,
Andrea Bocelli more Italian MEN
But none as great as Car-MAN
Brought thousands by his single HAND
Their souls he did WIN
God is so pleased and proud of HIM
Carman and dad have always BEEN
First on my list
OF ALL THE GREAT ITALIAN MEN!

# ST. PATRICK

(Christian name Maewyn Succat)
St. Patrick was a frightened soul
Cast aboard a slave ship
Put down in a hole
Captured by Irish raiders
And sold as a slave
He then became very brave
He ignored God his whole life
Until it became filled with strife
He turned to God in his darkest hour
Prayed he did and asked for power
Hundreds of prayers night and day
He taught us how to pray
After 6 years escaped for home
Where he didn't feel so alone
He then became a Holy man
To go back to that same land
He saved the whole country
Built churches and schools
That's why St. Patrick day rules!

Published in POEMS OF THE WORLD

Printed in the United States
By Bookmasters